Dawning Light:

Adoption

A 30-day
Dust2Diamond Devotional

Nancy Faltermeier & Kelly Sumner

SwordSower
Publishing

SwordSower Publishing
P.O. Box 98
Eastlake, Colorado 80614
www.swordsowerpublishing.com

SwordSower Logo – Jan Marie Wirth

Book Cover – Nancy Faltermeier

Editor – Juliet Kennedy

Publisher's Note: In this work of non-fiction, while stories are true, names and locales have been changed to protect identity. Any resemblance to actual people, living or dead, or to businesses, companies, events, or institutions, is completely coincidental. Although every precaution has been taken to verify the accuracy of the information contained herein, the author and publisher assume no responsibility for any errors or omissions. No liability is assumed for damages that may result from the use of information contained within.

Book Layout © 2016 BookDesignTemplates.com

Dawning Light: Adoption/Nancy Faltermeier & Kelly Sumner. -- 1st ed.
Print Edition ISBN 978-1-945391-04-0
Kindle Edition ISBN 978-1-945391-05-7

Dedication

We dedicate this book to all those brave souls considering or pursuing adoption. The road ahead may seem daunting, confusing, and challenging but it leads to a pot of golden rewards. May the Lord bless and guide you on your journey. In the end, you and a special child will be greatly blessed with the light of love.

Acknowledgments

This book shines brighter because of the input and guidance of our editor, Juliet Kennedy. We greatly appreciate your invaluable help and encouragement.

Our thanks go to all our critique partners whose insight helped us fill this book with practical wisdom and suggestions.

Contents

~ ◆ ~

Day 1 with Nancy

Faith Tested

The mind of man plans his way,
But the LORD directs his steps.
Proverbs 16:9

After two years of miscarriages and failed infertility treatments, Bob and Sue (not their real names) received a phone call from Jane, their caseworker at the adoption agency. She told them a birth mom had picked them out of their open adoption program. Ecstatic over the news, the couple prepared for their coming-home inspection and for their baby girl, who could arrive at any time.

A few nights later, news came that the birth mom was in labor. Bob and Sue were finally going to be parents. They raced to finish last minute preparations and stepped out the door to go to the hospital, pausing when the phone rang. Bob left Sue waiting on the driveway and ran back into the house to answer the call.

He returned to Sue, his eyes downcast. The birth mom changed her mind about the adoption.

Bob hugged Sue. "God has a baby out there for us. I know it."

Sue wished she had his confidence as she removed the car seat and diaper bag. They would not be parents that day.

Months passed before Bob and Sue received another call from Jane. "A birth mom selected you again. I believe this time it's going to be for real."

A week later, they met the twenty-something birth mom. She was married, but the baby she carried wasn't her husband's. Her husband would be away for an extended period of time, and she could give birth before he returned and didn't want him to know of her affair. They exchanged their personal information and scheduled another meeting.

They attended several meetings with the birth mom over the ensuing months and their hopes rose. The birth mother even gave them a sonogram picture of the baby. A little girl. She also requested their presence in the delivery room during the birth and asked them to pick the baby's name so she could call the baby by her name.

As the due date drew closer, family and friends threw Bob and Sue a baby shower. They were going to be parents.

With the baby's room now ready, they waited for "the call" that the birth mom was in labor. The call finally came, and they rushed to the hospital. Everything was coming together. The room oozed with excitement. Once their daughter emerged, the birth mom asked Bob to cut the umbilical cord. The medical staff allowed Sue to hold her daughter for a time before whisking the infant off to the nursery. The birth mom needed rest, and at the urging of nurses, Bob and Sue reluctantly returned home to get some sleep.

The next morning, at the first light of dawn, Bob and Sue got up. With flowers for the birth mom, an outfit for their daughter, and the car seat in tow, they returned to the hospital only to receive the news that the birth mom had changed her mind.

Why would God allow this to happen again?

Back at home, shower decorations sat on the mantel and baby items littered the living room, mocking their empty arms.

They might never be parents.

Deciding they needed to get away, they flew out the next morning for Disney World. Colorful flowers greeted them instead of the gray colors of winter. This would certainly be a distraction and a new experience for both of them. They had dreamed of sharing this adventure with children but that might never be.

The next day, the magical world around them brought only reminders they were childless. The number of families with small children only deepened their pain.

Bob's phone rang. He stepped out of the shop as Sue continued to explore the boutique. He returned with his face flushed with excitement. The birth mom had reconsidered and wanted them to pick up the baby as soon as possible.

They flew home that night and arrived at the adoption agency the next morning only to receive the unwelcome news that the birth mom had changed her mind yet again.

Another month went by. Bob and Sue were now convinced God had said "no" to their prayer for a child. The adoption process was too painful to continue. This would be the last month they would pay the adoption agency fee. This endeavor was nothing but a money pit.

Sue's mother called. She worked as an OB-GYN nurse. "We have a baby here that was born two days ago. The mother just deserted him. He's your baby. I just know it. Social Services is in touch with your adoption agency. I feel good about this."

As Sue hung up, she dismissed her mother's words, refusing to allow hope to rise. What did Mom know about adoption? She didn't tell Bob about the call. It was nothing more than her mother's pipe dream.

Two days later, the adoption agency called. "You have a son. The mom abandoned him at the hospital."

They hurried to the agency and met their son. God gave them a child that day—a child He picked just for them. It turned out Sue's mother was not only right, but she had rocked and talked to her grandchild on every break, believing God for him.

As we approach adoption, we must remember God is always in control. The adoption road can be just as bumpy as infertility as we try to make a match work. But it usually has a much higher success rate. While we must move forward in faith that the Lord will give us a child, it is He who does the choosing. Keep this in mind, because you may hit large potholes along the road. Don't let your heart be discouraged.

I'm so thankful that You, Lord, walk by our side as we pursue adoption. Help me not to lose faith if we hit bumps or potholes along the way. Remind me always that You are still in control, because You are mindful of us.

○✝♦✝○

God places every child in every home.

What dreams do you have for adoption? How do you imagine it will all come together?

_____

_____

_____

_____

_____

_____

_____

_____

_____

_____

_____

_____

_____

_____

_____

_____

_____

_____

_____

_____

_____

_____

_____

_____

_____

~ ◆ ~

Understanding Olive Plants

Your wife shall be like a fruitful vine within your house,
Your children like olive plants around your table.
Behold, for thus shall the man be blessed
Who fears the LORD.
Psalm 128:3–4

Olive groves don't only grow from seed. All it takes to plant an olive tree is a branch cut from another tree, good earth to plant it in, and, of course, water. You don't need a bag of olive pits to plant a grove of trees.

Just like God has made it possible to plant olive trees two ways, He has made families to form in two ways: by birth and by adoption.

We would never say a tree planted from a branch is not a *real* tree. So why would we get the idea that a family formed through adoption is not a *real* family? In God's eyes, they are one and the same.

When we give our lives to the Lord, He brings us into His family by adoption. What truer family can there be than God's family? Ephesians 1:5 says, "He predestined us to adoption as sons through Jesus Christ to Himself, according to the kind intention of His will".

It's so awesome, Lord, that You don't look at families formed by adoption as second-class families. Thank you. Help me to see things through Your eyes and give me Your mind on adoption.

○✝◆✝○

Families of adoption are true images of God's family.

What misconceptions do I have about adoption?

_____
_____
_____
_____
_____
_____
_____
_____
_____
_____
_____
_____
_____
_____
_____
_____
_____
_____
_____
_____
_____
_____
_____

~ ◆ ~

Day 3 with Kelly
Researching Adoption

Call to Me and I will answer you
And I will tell you great and mighty things,
which you do not know.
Jeremiah 33:3

Because I'm in a unique position of having been both adopted and having given up a child for adoption, I can speak to those considering adoption as a way to build your family. For starters, be realistic in what you are trying to accomplish. Recognize and accept your adopted child may not look like you, act like you, or enjoy the things you enjoy. Each child will be their own person, and will possibly bring a different way of thinking, and a new set of talents to the table.

Research. You really can't do too much of it. Call adoption agencies and ask lots of questions. If you don't like something, ask them about it, and if their answers don't work for you, look at other agencies.

Adoption can be a very rewarding experience if we do our homework. Pray and ask for God's for guidance. He will direct you to the right place.

Father, give me patience to do the research necessary to find the right fit for my family. I don't want to rush into anything not of You. Thank you for Your wisdom and amazing grace.

◦✝◆✝◦

Let go, and let God guide you.

What areas do I need to research and in what areas do I need to trust God more?

_____
_____
_____
_____
_____
_____
_____
_____
_____
_____
_____
_____
_____
_____
_____
_____
_____
_____
_____
_____
_____
_____
_____

~ ◆ ~

Day 4 with Nancy

Adoption:
Whose Idea Was It?

Blessed be the God and Father of our LORD Jesus Christ,
who has blessed us with every spiritual blessing
in the heavenly places in Christ,
just as He chose us in Him before the foundation of the world,
that we would be holy and blameless before Him.
*In love He predestined us to **adoption***
through Jesus Christ to himself,
according to the kind intention of His will…
Ephesians 1:3-5

We might think the concept of adoption came from man's plan to solve the problem of orphans. However, I would suggest the idea originated in the mind of God. In fact, the above scripture tells us God's plan for the adoption of wayward mankind was in place before the foundation of the world.

When considering adoption, unless we have experienced adoption previously in our family, it feels strange and perhaps un-natural. But if we have committed our lives to Jesus Christ, we realize that in the sight of God, we are adopted children.

We are far more acquainted with adoption than we realize.

In love, the Lord designed a plan to adopt us into the family of God. If we have asked the Lord to enter our hearts and have com-mitted to follow His ways, we can be confident we are part of the Royal Family of the Universe.

Thank You, Father, for Your awesome plan of adoption! I praise You for valuing my life enough to offer adoption to me. I am willing for You to become my Heavenly Father through the death of Your Son Jesus on the cross, to save me from the sin that separates me from You. Please forgive me for all the sinful and selfish things I've done and take control of my life. Teach me Your ways, Lord, and help me to honor You in all I do.

∘✝♦✝∘

Adoption originated in the mind of God.

If you prayed the above prayer for the first time and sincerely meant it, welcome to the family of God. Deepen your relationship with Him. Pour out your heart to Him on the lines below.

_____

_____

_____

_____

_____

_____

_____

_____

_____

_____

_____

~ ♦ ~

Day 5 with Nancy

God's Answer

For the needy will not always be forgotten,
Nor the hope of the afflicted perish forever.
Psalm 9:18

Most people who deal with infertility don't expect to encounter such a problem. We are surprised when we find ourselves with this unthinkable hitch in our plans. Why us? We may even shake our fists at God in protest.

The reality is we live in a broken, messed-up world. Man rebelled against our loving Creator, and we are left to deal with the fallout. But our Heavenly Father did not leave us alone.

Adoption is God's answer to two unthinkable dilemmas. Adoption fills the void in an infertile couple's life, and adoption provides a child with parents he or she desperately needs. Through it all, we gain a better understanding of God's encompassing love for us.

Trust is built through such circumstances. Cling to Him.

I don't understand what You are doing, Lord, but I choose to trust You. In spite of what I see, I believe You are in control and are working on my behalf. I will not doubt You but wait with expectation for the day when You bring all things together.

○✝♦✝○

He holds the answers to ALL of our problems.

What other problems in my life should I ask the Lord to help me with?

_____
_____
_____
_____
_____
_____
_____
_____
_____
_____
_____
_____
_____
_____
_____
_____
_____
_____
_____
_____
_____

~ ◆ ~

Day 6 with Nancy
Realistic Expectations

Love is patient, love is kind and is not jealous;
Love does not brag and is not arrogant,
does not act unbecomingly;
it does not seek its own, it is not provoked (easily angered),
does not take into account a wrong suffered,
does not rejoice in unrighteousness, but rejoices with the truth;
bears all things, believes all things, hopes all things, endures all
things.
Love never fails;
1 Corinthians 13:4–8a

It's natural for parents to hope their children will like and enjoy the same things they do. We want to share our love of music, sports, sewing, art, and our other passions with them. However, even in biological kids, interests vary. Children are not reproductions of ourselves. They are unique individuals.

While talents differ within a biological family, there are tendencies to gravitate toward similar interests. In adopted children, their bent may be foreign to you, but uniqueness is something to be celebrated and respected. God loves diversity.

We are all born with strengths and weaknesses in talents and character, and sometimes those strengths and weaknesses are passed from generation to generation. It's this bone of contention that frustrates many adoptive families. If one is strong in an area where the child struggles, misunderstanding the child's weakness can create walls and bitterness. We can be blinded by the battles we never had to fight and hold unrealistic expectations for the adoptive child. Love and awareness is the key to avoiding these pitfalls. The above scripture unlocks the wisdom to navigate around the bumps in the adoption road.

It's amazing how unique You've made each of us, Lord. Please remind me of this as I raise the children You give me, so that I can respect and celebrate the differences You have created.

∘✝◆✝∘

Variety flavors life.

What differences do I see in the members of my family?

_____

_____

_____

_____

_____

_____

_____

_____

_____

_____

_____

_____

_____

_____

_____

_____

_____

_____

_____

_____

_____

~◆~

Will I Be Up to The Task?

"Blessed is the man who trusts in the LORD
And whose trust is the LORD."
Jeremiah 17:7

I met a couple who adopted a child from China. I asked them what they worried the most about. Their answer was surprising. They said they feared they wouldn't be enough for their new daughter. They hoped their new daughter would love them as much as she would have loved her biological parents.

So many times we are concerned about other people's reactions and don't consider that they, too, have their own fears of inadequacy. If the Lord is putting us in an adoption situation, be assured He will provide us with the tools to do the job well. He has picked us for this job, because He knows we are up to the task if our dependence is upon Him.

Thank you, Lord, that you give me all I need to handle any job. Help me to rely on You and You alone when fears of inadequacy threaten to come in.

○✝◆✝○

With God, we are never alone.

What are my biggest fears about adoption?

_____
_____
_____
_____
_____
_____
_____
_____
_____
_____
_____
_____
_____
_____
_____
_____
_____
_____
_____
_____
_____

~ ◆ ~

Day 8 with Nancy
The People Who Adopt

*And we know that God causes all things to work together for good
to those who love God,
to those who are called according to His purpose.*
Romans 8:28

W hat kind of people adopt? Ordinary people like you and me. Adoption in the United States is quite common. Everyone knows someone who has been touched by adoption. You may have been adopted yourself.

What motivates people to adopt?

Most adoptive parents fit into one of four categories. The infertile couple comes to mind most often. However, there are others. Some people have always carried a desire to adopt. These types can be found taking in many children, both by adoption and by birth. Then there are those who take in foster children, bond with them, and fight to adopt them. The fourth are those who adopt a relative or friend's child when the child is orphaned.

It doesn't matter how the family comes together. God is the designer of them all. They are miracles put together with purpose and love.

Lord, You know my situation and the reason my spouse and I are considering adoption. Please go before us and straighten the path. We need You. Thank You for Your intimate love, care, and presence as we seek the way we should go.

∘✝◆✝∘
He has prepared a plan for each adoption story.

Who do I know who has adopted a child or who was adopted?
What stands out in their stories?

_____

_____

_____

_____

_____

_____

_____

_____

_____

_____

_____

_____

_____

_____

_____

_____

_____

_____

_____

_____

_____

_____

~ ◆ ~

Day 9 with Nancy

No Venture,
No Gain

It is better to take refuge in the LORD
Than to trust in man.
Psalm 118:8

Are you considering adoption, but have many questions and fears? Don't be afraid to ask the questions. You may not want to admit to some of the things you are feeling. One common fear that many people have is discovering, after the adoption is finalized, that they don't have love for a child they didn't give birth to.

Relax.

Most people find the fear vanishes the first minute they see the precious face of the child. Bonding tends to happen naturally as you take on the task of parenting. When something or someone is yours, you take ownership. Within the first couple of days, my son was as much mine as if I'd given birth to him.

Many adoptive parents also struggle with the fear the birth mother will change her mind. What a relief it was when the adoption agency relayed the news that the birth mom had given up her rights to our son. I would love to tell you that birth mothers never change their minds, but sometimes they do. Don't let this fear rob you of the greatest joys of parenting. Go forward with the belief that if it does, God didn't intend for the child to be part of your family from the beginning. Trust Him to use the trial you may endure in the process to develop you into the person He has planned for you to be. Don't allow the fear to paralyze you.

No matter what comes your way, the Lord will remain by your side. He's still there with comfort and guidance if you continue to put your trust in Him. Trust Him. He knows what He's doing.

I admit, Lord, there are fears in my heart about adoption. Help me to know You will be with us every step of the way. I realize adoption is a step of faith and an opportunity to follow You and to learn to trust You more. I put all my fears in Your hands and commit to go where You lead.

○✝◆✝○

Venturing into the unknown requires placing our trust in Him.

What are the fears I have about adoption?

_____
_____
_____
_____
_____
_____
_____
_____
_____
_____
_____
_____
_____
_____
_____

~ ◆ ~

Day 10 with Nancy
The Calling

Take heed to the ministry
which you have received in the LORD,
that you may fulfill it.
Colossians 4:17

If you are on the path to adoption and a child is placed into your home, you have been called into ministry. This ministry may not fit the usual definition, but when we take in someone else's child to raise as our own, it is nonetheless a ministry God ordained.

No matter what type of ministry a person has been called to, there is a story behind how that calling came to be. Unless you have always carried a desire in your heart to adopt, struggles with infertility often precede the adoption ministry. The Lord asks us to minister in as many different ways as there are souls on earth. He works individually with each of us.

If we recognize this, it will change how we approach adoption. What an honor for God to handpick us to raise a precious child of His. We also have a great responsibility to be the tool God uses to shape this young child into the adult the Father can use for His purposes.

Don't ever feel like you're settling for second best or that you've been forced into adoption because you didn't measure up to birth your own biological children. The truth is you've been handpicked for the mission before you. God knows your potential. He's not just giving you a child. He's giving you a ministry. He sees that if you're submitted to Him, you'll have the "right stuff" for the job. Fulfill your ministry!

Thank You, Lord, for calling me into a special ministry. Give me wisdom for the task, and help me accomplish all that You would have me do. I submit to Your will and look forward to the exciting things You have for me in the future. I am honored.

∘✝◆✝∘

Adoption is full-time ministry.

What areas do I need to work on to be prepared for the ministry the Lord is calling me to?

_____

_____

_____

_____

_____

_____

_____

_____

_____

_____

_____

_____

_____

_____

_____

_____

_____

_____

~ ◆ ~

Day 11 with Kelly
The Unknown

Be anxious for nothing,
but in everything by prayer and supplication with thanksgiving
let your requests be made known to God.
And the peace of God, which surpasses all comprehension,
will guard your hearts and your minds in Christ Jesus.
Philippians 4:6–7

When you adopt a child, you are dealing with the unknown. Will the child be healthy? Will she blend in with your family? What if he has special needs? There are many questions when considering adoption and too few answers.

The birth mother has many questions, too. Will this family love her child? Will they treat her child as part of the family? Both adoptive and birth parents are dealing with questions of the unknown.

So how do we manage all of the uncertainties of adoption?

Pray and trust God for your situation that He will give you the right child.

As we walk through these uncertainties, our faith in God is a must. This is an opportunity to grow in faith. Don't be frightened away.

Lord, the unknown can seem scary. I am often frightened by what I don't know or can't explain. Sometimes, Father, the unknown can be amazing and wonderful, like discovering a new galaxy or a new part of the ocean. Help me not to fear the unknown but to embrace it and to trust you, Lord. When you are with me, no one can stand against me.

∘✝◆✝∘

God knows the unknown.

What fears of the unknown can I give to God?

_____

_____

_____

_____

_____

_____

_____

_____

_____

_____

_____

_____

_____

_____

_____

_____

_____

_____

_____

_____

~ ♦ ~

Day 12 with Nancy

True Religion

*Pure and undefiled religion
in the sight of our God and Father is this:
to visit orphans and widows in their distress,
and to keep oneself unstained by the world.*
James 1:27

You may be wondering right now, "Does God want us to adopt?" I can't tell you the answer specifically for your situation. However, as you search for this answer, you might want to consider the above verse from James 1:27 and the following verses:

"Then the King will say to those on His right, 'Come, you who are blessed of My Father, inherit the kingdom prepared for you from the foundation of the world. For I was hungry, and you gave Me something to eat; I was thirsty, and you gave Me something to drink; I was a stranger, and you invited Me in; naked, you clothed Me; I was sick, and you visited Me; I was in prison, and you came to Me.' Then the righteous will answer Him, 'LORD, when did we see You hungry, and feed You, or thirsty, and give You something to drink? And when did we see You a stranger, and invite You in, or naked, and clothe You? When did we see You sick, or in prison, and come to You?' The King will answer and say to them, 'Truly I say to you, to the extent

that you did it to one of these brothers of
Mine, even the least of them, you did it to
Me.'" (Matthew 25:34–40)

I believe these two scriptures—James 1:27 and Matthew 25:34-40—are linked, and I can't help but believe orphans and children in need of good homes fall into the category of "the least of these". What an honor it would be for Jesus to become a part of our families. We'd have the privilege to serve Him in practical ways daily. According to the verses above, adoption provides us this opportunity.

This gives us the correct focus on adoption. It's not about what we are providing for a child in need, but the fact we now have an honored guest living in our homes.

Thank You, Jesus, for the opportunities You give me to serve You. Help me to honor You in all I do. Open my eyes to the needs around me, and help me do what I can to meet those needs. Please give my spouse and me Your wisdom on adoption.

○✝◆✝○

The Lord is always mindful of the "least of these".

In what ways can I serve the Lord now and in the future?

_____

_____

_____

_____

_____

_____

~ ◆ ~

Day 13 with Nancy
The Cost of Adoption

And my God will supply all your needs
according to His riches in glory in Christ Jesus.
Philippians 4:19

When we dip our toes into the waters of adoption, we often feel as though we've stepped into a bucket of frigid water. We recoil with "sticker shock". Why, we ask, is adopting so expensive? This question can be answered in many ways, depending on the type of adoption we pursue and the adoption agency we use.

When we pursued adoption, foreign adoptions were more expensive due to travel costs and the amount of time required to stay in the country. Those expenses came before agency, legal, and foreign country fees, which raised the total final cost.

The Lord brought us to the open adoption door, but still thousands of dollars were needed. Agencies must pay staff and often provide counseling to unwed mothers for free, who, in many cases, decide to keep their babies.

Many couples have already spent a fortune on infertility treatments. Adoption may now be the only option left to them. They may feel the Lord has brought them to this juncture to welcome a needy child into their home, except for the costs involved.

Couples may be tempted to put all the costs on credit. Some may be able to do this, knowing they can pay it off in a short amount of time, but if that is not the case, I'd advise you to set as much as possible aside to cover costs. If you can keep out of debt, you will be better off when the child becomes part of your family.

Follow what's in your heart and trust the Lord to supply the funds needed to accomplish the goal. Start a savings account for adoption and look to Him to fill it with the necessary finances. Be creative in how you can fill that account. Is there a side job you can do? Do you have a talent that you could use to make extra cash? Is there something worth a chunk of money sitting unused that you could sell?

I owned a top-of-the-line knitting machine I no longer used. I sold it for a fair-sized amount. In another instance, our neighbor backed into our car, and instead of spending the insurance money to repair the dent, we put it into our adoption savings.

The bottom line is this: If the Lord wants to build your family through adoption, He will supply the money. Trust Him. Our God is a miracle worker.

You know what my bank statement looks like, Lord. Help me not to be discouraged by my lack. You own "the cattle upon a thousand hills." Show me what things I can do to set aside money for this purpose. Thank You for meeting all our needs.

º✝◆✝º

**Keeping our eyes on Him for what we need,
keeps our eyes off our lack.**

What things can I do to set aside money toward adopting?

_____

_____

_____

_____

_____

_____

_____

~ ◆ ~

Day 14 with Nancy
Genes Vs. Influence

Train up a child in the way he should go,
Even when he is old he will not depart from it.
Proverbs 22:6

Some people resist the idea of adoption, because they won't be able to pass on their genes to their child. I will agree there is an element of loss, but it's not everything. It's natural to wonder what your birth child would have looked like, but how important is it really? Once a child is yours, he or she belongs to you. I have both biological and adopted children. I can assure you, it matters little.

It's important to move past this loss and advance toward adoption. In reality, our influence upon the child shapes them far more than their genes. The values we give our child, whether adopted or not, remain the most important things a parent can impart.

What does God care about most?

I believe godly influence is at the top of His list. If adoptive parents give their child love, acceptance, and a good set of God-fearing values, they will have put into them and contributed more than genes could have ever accomplished.

I pray now, Lord, for wisdom. Help my spouse and me to raise whatever child or children You give us to know, honor, and live for You. Your values are the most important thing we can pass on to our children. Remind me of this as we continue our quest for children, and develop me into the person You desire me to be.

∘✝◆✝∘

Passing on the Lord's ways is passing on eternal life.

What values are important for you to pass on to your child?

_____
_____
_____
_____
_____
_____
_____
_____
_____
_____
_____
_____
_____
_____
_____
_____
_____
_____
_____
_____
_____
_____
_____
_____
_____
_____

~ ◆ ~

Day 15 with Kelly
Am I Ready to Adopt?

Prepare your work outside
and make it ready for yourself in the field;
afterwards, then, build your house.
Proverbs 24:27

When we are considering adoption, we must ask ourselves what we hope to gain.

Am I ready to love someone as my own flesh and blood?

Am I prepared to face family members who don't feel the same way I do?

Am I willing to accept that there is no way to predict if a child will have special needs?

These are just a few of the questions we need to explore within ourselves. If you can answer yes to these questions, you are on your way to adoption. This topic is addressed in more depth in our book *Entwined by Adoption: Our Story of Infertility, Teen Pregnancy, and Faith.* I pray God opens the door of adoption to you. Be sure to pray about the option and allow the Lord to do a work in your life.

Help me, Father, to search my heart to know if adoption is truly Your will for my life. Adoption is a noble cause but not for everyone. I pray for the wisdom to know if I am ready to adopt.

◦✝◆✝◦

Your rest is in God.

Take time to answer the three questions listed above. Have I answered all these questions truthfully?

_____
_____
_____
_____
_____
_____
_____
_____
_____
_____
_____
_____
_____
_____
_____
_____
_____
_____
_____
_____
_____
_____
_____
_____
_____

~ ◆ ~

Day 16 with Nancy
Time to Grieve

My soul weeps because of grief;
Strengthen me according to Your word.
Psalm 119:28

When my husband and I sat down to fill out the application to adopt, we ended up quarreling. There was no good reason. The true issue at hand was we hadn't taken the time to grieve our invisible loss. The act of filling out that form broke open the wounds we carried but could not see. It brought us to the raw reality that the child we had envisioned to look like us, act like us, and carry our genes would not be.

We experienced the death of a dream.

People on the outside don't recognize the loss. It's unseen but real. The pain tells you so. Don't be caught in the trap of denying its existence. Take time to set your dream free. Give those unmet hopes to the Lord. I suggest buying an object, like a toy boat or a helium balloon. Write a farewell to your dream, attach the note to the object, and let the wind, river, or ocean carry the letter away. Watch it leave you. Then, in prayer, write yourself a new dream which includes an adopted child or two. Set your course toward the goal, and anticipate the joys awaiting you.

Help me, Jesus, to let go of the dream of having a biological child. I give the dream to You, knowing You hold my future in Your hand. Please replace the dream I'm releasing to You with Your dream for us. I thank You for Your presence in our struggle.

∘✝◆✝∘

When given to Him, He turns our tears to rivers of joy.

What is the unmet dream in my life? Ask the Lord for His dream for you, and write it down.

_____
_____
_____
_____
_____
_____
_____
_____
_____
_____
_____
_____
_____
_____
_____
_____
_____
_____
_____
_____
_____
_____

~ ◆ ~

Day 17 with Nancy

The Lord
As Our Example

But when the fullness of the time came,
God sent forth His Son,
born of a woman, born under the law,
so that He might redeem those who were under the law,
that we might receive the adoption as sons.
Galatians 4:4–5

M any couples today are opting to adopt dogs or cats as their children, thinking someday they will have "enough" money for kids. Others buy into this idea, because they don't want to be "bothered" with raising a child. I would encourage a couple struggling with infertility not to settle for this solution. That plan only leads down a dark hole.

Yes, it's easier but much less fulfilling. Fulfillment comes from conquering challenges. Children do bring trouble, but they also bring joy and love. Some say the same could be said for a dog. A child, however, is an eternal being, someone of value for you to invest your life in. They grow up to be somebody with hopes and dreams and accomplishments of their own. An animal stays the same animal they've always been, looking for the next meal, walk, or belly rub.

A greater growth happens for parents by raising children. The family is God's laboratory to grow us into the people He wants us to be. With so many children in desperate need of a loving and stable home, it's shortsighted.

We need to follow God's lead. He did the hard thing. He sent His only begotten Son to die in our place. What was His purpose? His intention was adoption. He could then adopt us as His own.

Direct us, Lord, in the way we should go. Help us to follow You wherever You lead. While I know You care for all of Your creation and animals should be well-treated, You gave Your life for mankind. Help me to know Your heart on these matters.

∘✝◆✝∘

**While God cares for all His creation,
He gave His Son for mankind.**

Which solution would bring me the most fulfillment?

_____
_____
_____
_____
_____
_____
_____
_____
_____
_____
_____
_____

~ ◆ ~

Day 18 with Nancy

What's in A Name?

"With this the words of the Prophets agree,
just as it is written, 'After these things I will return,
I will rebuild the and tabernacle of David which has fallen,
And I will rebuild its ruins, and I will restore it,
So that the rest of mankind may seek the LORD,
*And all the Gentiles **who are called by My name,***
says the LORD, who makes these things known from long ago.'"
Acts 15:15–18

When a child is adopted, one of the first things that happens is the child is given a new name. The child receives the name of the adoptive parents. What does this mean? It means the child is now yours and belongs to no other. Legally, all the requirements have been met, and that new name binds the child to you forever.

The child is yours—your heir, your chosen one. The adopted son or daughter will be called by your name. With the name change, you become responsible to feed, clothe, shelter, and, most of all, love the child.

What a great example of the things God has done for us. If we come to Him for help, He will take us in, adopt us, make us His own, and give us a new name—His name.

Heavenly Father, I am so grateful You made me Your child. What an awesome opportunity You have given me in giving me Your name. Help me honor You and become more like You. Thank You, Lord.

∘✝◆✝∘

**The blood-bought children of God
are given the family name *Christians*.**

What are some ways I can show the Lord how thankful I am for
His adoption of me?

_____
_____
_____
_____
_____
_____
_____
_____
_____
_____
_____
_____
_____
_____
_____
_____
_____
_____
_____
_____
_____
_____
_____

~ ◆ ~

Day 19 with Kelly
Birth Mom, Chooses Adoption

Let us not lose heart in doing good, for in due
time we will reap if we do not grow weary.
Galatians 6:9

One question I am asked frequently is why did I choose an adoption plan for my child? It wasn't an easy decision, and I waffled back and forth a lot. The choice ultimately came down to whether I could provide for my child. My child deserved a stable family life, and at seventeen, I could barely take care of myself, let alone a child. I wanted him to have the best future I could give him with two parents that loved him. I knew he would have the best chance at that if I chose an adoption plan.

This gut-wrenching choice does not come easy, but most adoption agencies provide counseling, and I was better prepared because of their efforts. People prayed for me as well. These prayers held me up through those hard times.

If you are looking to adopt a baby, pray for the birth mother. This is a tough time for her, and your prayers might be the ones that help her through the decision.

Lord, help me to be mindful of others. I don't always know what people are going through or what they are facing. Adoption is a beautiful and wonderful thing, but never let me forget the pain the birth mother goes through in making this decision. Thank you for all the ones who have made this choice, and bless them, Father.

◦†◆†◦

Your prayers may be the strength someone needs.

How do I think it feels to a birth mother who must consider adoption? Write a detailed description.

_____

_____

_____

_____

_____

_____

_____

_____

_____

_____

_____

_____

_____

_____

_____

_____

_____

_____

_____

_____

_____

_____

_____

~ ♦ ~

Day 20 with Nancy
Adopt with Honesty

I will make justice the measuring line
and righteousness the level;
Then hail will sweep away the refuge of lies,
And the waters will overflow the secret place.
Isaiah 28:17

I've heard of and met people who are reluctant to tell their adopted child that he or she is adopted. This is my advice: Don't go down that road. It's lying, and deceit never has a good result. Resist the temptation.

Pretending we have given birth to our child will eventually blow up when the child finds out that is not true. This most assuredly will damage our relationship with our child.

I'm not saying we must reveal to everyone our child is adopted, but when it is in the best interest of the child, we shouldn't be afraid to tell him or her.

My son has always been tall for his age, and I'm a short lady. Mere acquaintances would question why that was. They were being nosey, and there was no reason for me to give them information. I smiled and said, "His father is much taller than I am." This was the truth and would shut the conversation down.

Ask the Lord for wisdom on these matters, and He will give it. Remember, though, that honesty is paramount. Many trials are caused by telling untruths. Let's save ourselves from these heartbreaks.

Help me, Lord, to be truthful in all things. Deceit has destroyed many lives and families. I ask You to set a guard over my mouth to protect me from speaking the words of the enemy for he is the father of lies. I thank You, Father, for cleansing me from all unrighteousness and deception.

∘✝◆✝∘

We never go wrong with God and others if we tell the truth.

What strategy can I put in place to keep honesty paramount in our adoption plan?

_____
_____
_____
_____
_____
_____
_____
_____
_____
_____
_____
_____
_____
_____
_____
_____
_____
_____
_____
_____

~◆~

Day 21 with Nancy

The Special Child

(Jesus) said to them,
"Whoever receives this child in My name receives Me,
and whoever receives Me receives Him who sent me;
for the one who is least among all of you, this is the one who is
great."
Luke 9:48

Though scripture doesn't tell us, I wouldn't be surprised to find out the little child in the above verse was a child with some sort of disability. The least among us could be described many different ways, but children with disabilities are certainly among them, particularly in biblical times.

Prospective parents often fear that their child will be born with a disability or genetic disease. This is across the board, whether the child is of birth or adoption. We all want our children to be born "normal" and in perfect health. This, I believe, comes out of the natural, protective instinct God has given to mankind and most species. We want the best for our offspring.

Unfortunately, adoptive parents sometimes disrupt an adoption, because they discovered the adoptive child had a disability. How sad for the child. Life doesn't come with guarantees.

When we approach adoption, we would do well to hold the same attitude as if the child was a natural born child: Trust God. The Lord is always in control, and if He sees fit to give us a child with a disability, it is because He views us as the best parents to raise the child with love and honor. Yes, it is a harder task, but the Father believes that with His help, you are up to the task. Remember, by welcoming these children into our homes, we are welcoming Jesus Himself.

I am so grateful, Father, that You are in control. It is in my heart for all the children You give me to be normal and healthy. If, however, You choose to give my spouse and me a child with special needs, please give us the same love You have for the child. I thank You, Lord, that my strength is found in You.

○✝◆✝○

When we honor the least among us, we honor Jesus.

In what ways can I prepare my heart to love a child with special needs?

_____
_____
_____
_____
_____
_____
_____
_____
_____
_____
_____
_____
_____
_____
_____
_____
_____
_____
_____

~ ◆ ~

Day 22 with Nancy

The Unseen Cost of Parenthood

Offer the sacrifices of righteousness,
And trust in the LORD.
Psalm 4:5

Most people who are serious about adopting have counted the financial cost of the process. Many overlook the cost of lifestyle changes a parent must make. The longer we have been childless, the more we tend to fill our lives with things of pleasure.

Many couples who have longed for a child usually are ready to make whatever adjustments are required. Any parent will tell you kids changed their lives, and their children demanded their focus and energy. Their lives are no longer only about themselves but their children as well.

When a birth child enters the family, the change can take a more gradual pace. With nine months of pregnancy, the parents prepare for an infant. Although they may face interruptions in sleep for feedings, the child stays in one place because he or she isn't mobile yet.

It would be wise for adoptive parents to take into consideration the age of the child they are adopting and plan accordingly. If a couple is adopting from a foreign country, usually the child is older, and quite possibly, a toddler. This will be a steeper adjustment, because the child has reached an active stage of life and is trying to process what just happened to him or her.

The key here is preparation. Expect your extra activities may have to take a backseat for a while. Talk to the Lord about what may have to go, and be willing to step away from those activities He shows you. If the first year or so is devoted to bonding with the child, establishing a new family life, and learning selflessness, we can't go wrong.

I praise You, Father, because You know all things. You know me, my spouse, and the child or children You are placing into our home. Please prepare me and everyone involved for this coming transition. I'm so grateful You are walking this road with us. Thank You.

○✝◆✝○

A selfless attitude invites peace into our homes.

What are the things I may have to give up for a while to become a parent?

_____

_____

_____

_____

_____

_____

_____

_____

_____

_____

_____

_____

_____

_____

~ ◆ ~

Day 23 with Kelly

Stereotyping Birth Mothers

This is My commandment,
that you love one another, just as I have loved you.
Greater love has no one than this,
that one lay down his life for his friends.
John 15:12

A common misconception I often hear is that birth mothers are promiscuous, or poor and possibly homeless, or drug addicts. What people don't understand is that a birth mother could be your neighbor's daughter living next door to you.

I was that girl—a good student and an athlete. I attended church and came from a middle-class family.

We should erase any preconceived notions about who we think the birth mother is and accept her for what she is doing for us. None of us is perfect, and all of us have messed up in one way or another. We are imperfect beings in an imperfect world. It's easy to form stereotypes; it's not so easy to open your heart and see a person the way God sees him or her.

Remember, the birth mother doesn't know you, yet she is willing to give you something so precious—a gift the Lord highly values. She places not only her infant but also her trust in you to take good care of her child. Your child. Perhaps instead of hanging onto stereotypes, pray for her. You might consider volunteering at a local crisis pregnancy center where you could meet some actual birth moms. You may discover they aren't really so different from you as you might have thought.

Lord, we truly are imperfect beings. Without You, all hope would be lost. Thank You for laying it on the hearts of birth mothers to give up their children for adoption. Please help me to not stereotype them but instead see them through Your eyes, Father.

∘✝◆✝∘

In a perfect world, everyone would see us as God sees us.

What opinions have I formed about what a birthmother is? How can I change my view?

_____
_____
_____
_____
_____
_____
_____
_____
_____
_____
_____
_____
_____
_____
_____
_____

~ ◆ ~

Day 24 with Nancy
God's Purposes

And not only this, but there was Rebekah also,
when she had conceived twins by one man, our father Isaac;
for though the twins were not yet born
and had not done anything good or bad,
so that God's purpose according to His choice would stand,
not because of works but because of Him who calls,
it was said to her,
"THE OLDER WILL SERVE THE YOUNGER."
Romans 9:10–12

As God calls parents to adopt, He places adoptee children according to His purposes. Like the above scripture shows, the Lord sometimes places a call on people before they are born. We may not always see His purposes and understand His reasoning, but in the end, all will come to light.

A study of scripture bears this out, and there are many examples. Adoption often marks someone for a special calling in scripture, such as Moses. Space doesn't allow me to go deep into this subject, but if you want to read more, I have written all about it in the book *Entwined by Adoption: Our Story of Infertility, Teen Pregnancy, and Faith.*

Adoption always rises from what we perceive as negative circumstances. So why would the Lord use those times to surround someone's birth and call? When we look at the big picture through God's eyes, we see that adoption is part of the molding process for the child's calling.

We find a window into the Father's thinking in the story of Joseph. Joseph lost his mother at a fairly young age, which made his upbringing different. After his brothers sold him into slavery and then he rose to power as the second in command of all Egypt, he

45

was reconciled to his brothers. Joseph said, "As for you, you meant evil against me, but God meant it for good in order to bring about this present result, to preserve many people alive" (Genesis 50:20).

Though the negative elements exist in an adoption's formation, God means it for good.

You are faithful, Father, to each one of us involved in adoption. Thank You for the children of special calling You are placing in my home. Please provide the wisdom to be the willing tool in Your hand.

◦✝◆✝◦

God uses adoption for His purposes.

How do I think God will use me and my spouse in our adopted child's life?

_____
_____
_____
_____
_____
_____
_____
_____
_____
_____
_____
_____
_____
_____

~ ◆ ~

Day 25 with Kelly
What is Cradle Care?

"… for the LORD your God is the one who goes with you.
He will not fail you or forsake you."
Deuteronomy 31:6

C radle care is a foster home a child goes to after release from the hospital. I chose to put my child in cradle care after my hospital stay to make sure adoption was really what I wanted. I was also in a foster home as a newborn, and I've enjoyed reading through some of the notes my foster mother wrote about me. I feel her love for me through her words. It must take amazing people to care for newborns and not get attached.

My plan after giving birth to my son was to put him in cradle care for two weeks. I left myself options so I would know I was making the right choice. It ended up being shorter than two weeks because I knew, after being home for a day, that adoption was the best option for him. I'm so grateful for families who open up their homes to babies in order to give time to young mothers to be sure they are making the correct decision. Cradle care is also a great way for the adoptive families to come and visit the child and to see how they get on with the newborn.

Pray for your new child's smooth transition from the birth mom to cradle care and from cradle care to your home. Even for babies, these moves can still be very stressful.

The adoptive mother of my son says he had severe separation anxiety until he was two years of age. Now is the time to start praying over your future child.

Lord, thank you for all the families who volunteer to become cradle care homes. I can't imagine how hard it would be to not get attached. Thank you for the special calling on their lives You have given them. Thank you also that such a place exists for babies to go so birth moms can decide what to do. Be with these mothers and children as they go through this difficult time.

∘✝◆✝∘

The one who casts all cares to God knows God cares.

What do I think about cradle care now?

_____
_____
_____
_____
_____
_____
_____
_____
_____
_____
_____
_____
_____
_____
_____
_____
_____
_____
_____
_____
_____

~ ◆ ~

Day 26 with Nancy

I'm What???

*I solemnly charge you in the presence of God
and of Christ Jesus and of His chosen angels,
to maintain these principles without bias,
doing nothing in a spirit of partiality.*
1 Timothy 5:21

We've all heard stories of couples who have adopted and then discovered they are expecting a biological child. I know several people this has happened to. The Lord has a sense of humor, but He also has His purpose in everything He does. Some couples have biological children but still have the God-given desire to adopt. Whatever the situation, we need to prepare ourselves with a strategy for such an occurrence.

My father's first wife passed away when their two children were still very young. When he married my mother and I was born, they set up family "rules" to try to equal the playing field. They made sure all of us siblings received equal shares. If a box of six popsicles was purchased and brought home, we were informed that we could each have two. Once we had eaten our share, we didn't get anymore. This may seem, to some, as a legalistic approach, but it did work.

Since I have one biological child and one adopted, I am very intentional to have the same amount of Christmas presents under the tree and spend similar amounts. The last thing I want is for my son to feel like he is not a full part of the family.

It's very important that the adopted child feels he belongs and is accepted. God is not a God of partiality. He loves us all, shows us all mercy, and disciplines us all when we go astray. Yet, He works with each of us differently according to our unique personalities and perceptions, but He never compromises His standards. Once again, the Lord is our example. We will do well if we follow His lead.

If You give us both biological and adopted children, Lord, please give me wisdom and understanding to manage our family in a way where all our children feel they belong. Help me not to pick favorites or be partial to one child over another. I thank You that, if we are given such gifts, each child will have been placed in our home by You.

o✝◆✝o

Showing partiality sows discord.

If I am blessed with both biological and adopted children, what strategies can I put in place that will make everyone feel like an equal part of the family?

_____
_____
_____
_____
_____
_____
_____
_____
_____
_____
_____
_____

~◆~

Day 27 with Nancy

When A Child
Should Be Told

Lovingkindness and truth have met together;
Righteousness and peace have kissed each other.
Psalm 85:10

The fact that a child is adopted should never be hidden. It's good for the child to hear the word adoption, even as a baby. You don't want to overdo it, but mention the fact when it's natural. When my son was a baby, I would tell him, "I'm glad we adopted you."

Frame the concept as a good thing. Don't leave the child with the impression there is something wrong with adoption, or that they should be embarrassed about how they became part of the family.

Our adoption was an open one, and most years, we would get together with Kelly's family around my son's birthday. Even when he was very young, I explained to him that he came out of Kelly's tummy and that God blessed him, because he had two families that loved him.

This approach prevents the child from enduring unnecessary trauma when they find out the truth. My son tells me he always felt like adoption was a natural occurrence. He doesn't remember "a moment" when he realized he had been adopted. He just always knew. Because of this, he's not been left with unanswered questions.

If You lead me into adoption, Lord, give me the wisdom and
correct insight of the things that come up for an adopted child. I'm

so thankful I won't have to do this alone. Please be by my side every step of the way.

◦✝◆✝◦

Truth given with love and kindness is the right thing to do, which in turn brings peace.

What things can I plan to do to help my adopted child feel good about adoption?

_____
_____
_____
_____
_____
_____
_____
_____
_____
_____
_____
_____
_____
_____
_____
_____
_____
_____
_____

~ ◆ ~

Day 28 with Nancy
The Inheritance

Blessed be the God and Father of our LORD Jesus Christ,
who according to His great mercy has caused us to be born again
to a living hope
through the resurrection of Jesus Christ from the dead,
to obtain an inheritance which is imperishable and undefiled and
will not fade away, reserved in heaven for you,
1 Peter 1:3-4

S ome parents with both biological and adopted children have chosen not to include their adopted children in their inheritance. This is a huge mistake.

It's hard to lose a parent, even if the child is an adult. But it is devastating to an adopted child to discover that they were not considered a full part of the family. They will feel betrayed and not one of your "real" children. Remember, you are their only real family.

This type of decision leaves destruction in its wake. It divides the children, bringing greater stress into an already difficult situation. The biological children may feel guilty, while the adopted child may feel resentment. It's best for all who are left behind to get equal shares of the inheritance.

God is our example. He not only has adopted us as His children through Jesus, but has given all His children an inheritance. We will rule and reign with Christ. Thank you, Heavenly Father!

You have given me an eternal inheritance, Lord. Thank You,
Father. Show me practical ways I can give my adopted children an

inheritance equal to that which I give to any biological children we may have. I appreciate that You have shown us Your heart on the matter.

○✝◆✝○

If we follow the Lord's example, we will not leave trouble in our wake.

Make an inheritance plan for all your future children.

_____
_____
_____
_____
_____
_____
_____
_____
_____
_____
_____
_____
_____
_____
_____
_____
_____
_____
_____

~◆~

Searching with God For Birth Parents

Let me hear Your lovingkindness in the morning;
For I trust in You;
Teach me the way in which I should walk;
For to you I lift up my soul.
Psalm 143:8

I have been on two sides of the adoption triangle. I released my son for adoption, and I, too, was adopted. I get asked often about whether I'm going to try to find my biological parents. I think about this often, but my answer varies from day to day. My biological mother was young when she gave birth to me, and my adoption papers say her family didn't know about the pregnancy.

I only have a few facts from my adoption papers and really not much of a family medical history to go on. Sometimes I think it would be great to know where I come from, but on other days, I wonder if I want to complicate my life even more than it already is.

Adoptive parents should realize most adopted children carry this hole in their hearts, because it feels like a piece of them is missing. My adoptive family will always be my family. For most adoptees, finding their birth parents has nothing to do with disowning the family that raised them. It's about feeling complete. God has given us the capacity to love without bounds. Adoptees don't have to quit loving their family to love their family of birth. If your adopted child desires to find their birth parents, support them. Trust the Lord. He may enlarge your family with extra blessings.

I know who I am in God. I'm a part of His family, and that is all that really matters. A couple years ago, I put my profile on every adoption search website. If my biological family searches for me, they will surely find me. I've left it up to God. He knows my biological family's situation, and He knows mine. I've put my trust in Him. I trust you will, too.

Lord, I put my trust in You. I don't know where the path will lead, but I know that You know, and that is enough for me. Give me wisdom each day to trust You.

∘✝◆✝∘

God is the healer of my heart.

What grief, fear, and heartache can I give to the Lord?

_____
_____
_____
_____
_____
_____
_____
_____
_____
_____
_____
_____
_____
_____
_____

~ ◆ ~

Day 30 with Nancy
Finding Birth Parents

We know love by this,
That He laid down His life for us;
and we ought to lay down our lives for the brethren.
1 John 3:16

On a Christian TV program, I discovered a story that piqued my interest into my own family tree. The host of the show interviewed a Jewish-Christian man from Germany who had survived the Holocaust. As a young child, this man was raised in a Christian home of Jewish origin that was part of a small denomination.

His story horrified me. As Nazism grew, the church they attended didn't want them to fellowship with their congregation anymore. The family moved to another church, but they didn't want them either. The Nazis didn't care in the least that this family was Christian, and none of their "Christian friends" were willing to hide them, so they were hauled off to a death camp. This man was the sole survivor of his family.

What caught my interest the most was the man's last name. It was my maiden name. But not only that, my ancestors came from Germany with strong ties to the same small denomination. Could there be a Jewish heritage in my family tree? Did they abandon their Jewishness when they came to the New World? Since they were Christians, did they feel it prudent for their descendants to keep the heritage from them? I don't know but would still like to research to find out.

So why did I tell you this story? I'm not adopted, but I still possess a healthy curiosity about my family tree. If I feel this way about the distant past of my family, how much more would adopted children be curious about their biological stories?

If I discovered I belong to Abraham's descendants, would I abandon my Christian faith? Never. My faith is who I am. In most cases, an adopted child would never abandon the family he or she is bonded to.

Some parents with adopted children live in fear of the biological parents, believing that they will usurp their place as the parent. What will they do if their child grows up and searches for his or her birth family?

This is my advice: Do what love demands. If Jesus loved us enough to lay down His life for us, can't we lay down our fears to support our child's need?

I'm not sure, Lord, what I would do in that situation. Help me to be willing to love my child beyond my fears and to trust You with every situation that may arise.

◦✝◆✝◦

Love sometimes requires us to do the hard thing.

What can I plan to do if my adopted child wants to search for his or her birth parents?

_____
_____
_____
_____
_____
_____
_____
_____
_____

Other Books by These Authors

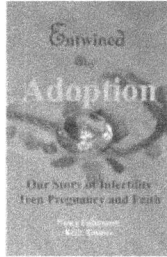

Entwined by Adoption
Our Story of Infertility, Teen Pregnancy and Faith
Adoption is the cord entwined by His design.

PART ONE

Shattered dreams of motherhood lay in Nancy's heart, bludgeoned by infertility. Would she ever feel whole?

The darkness of teen pregnancy engulfed Kelly, swallowing her into the pit of hopelessness. Pregnant? She couldn't be. Her family might disown her.

Could these two women hold the answer to each other's prayers? In this heart wrenching and miraculous, true story of adoption, Kelly and Nancy team up to share how God mends hearts to see the light again.

This book delivers far more than just their story. They present two study journals packed full of practical tips, and answers many questions such as:

PART TWO
- Why does God allow infertility?
- Is infertility a punishment?
- What does the Bible say about infertility and adoption?
- Should I adopt?
- Am I ready to adopt?

PART THREE
- I'm pregnant. Now what?
- Is my life ruined?
- As a parent of a pregnant teen, what should I do?

And much, much more . . .

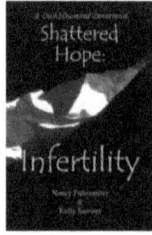

Shattered Hope: Infertility

This 30-day Dust2Diamond Devotional will take you on a journey through the spiritual and practical issues of infertility, while focusing on the presence of God in your life.

Diamonds: Tale of Trial

Out of the depths of hardship and pain, diamonds rise.

Have you experienced disappointment, rejection, or pain? Do you wonder if you've been forgotten, like no one cares?

Where is God in the midst of our struggles? What good can come from them?

In this book, we take a look at Joseph's life through the analogy of a gem quality diamond's journey. Beginning as something ugly and black, it turns, through great hardship, into a wondrous beauty that reflects His light in prisms of color.

Visit us at: www.fromdust2diamonds.com

Our Blog: dust2diamonds.wordpress.com

If you have found this book to be helpful, we would love to hear about it. Please write to us at dust2diamonds1@gmail.com. May God bless you on this journey.

ABOUT THE AUTHORS

From Dust2Diamond Authors
Kelly Sumner and Nancy Faltermeier

Kelly Sumner is a teacher with experience in both public and private schools. Her involvement in the teen pregnancy clinic has inspired her to write about her experience as a teenage birth mother. She has published *Broken Dreams Made Whole* in *Apraxia Now* magazine. A magazine devoted to parents of children unable to speak.

She devotes her time to teaching her own preschool, writing fiction for women, young adults, and suspense lovers. Residing in gorgeous Colorado, Kelly lives with her husband, two children, a dog, and a conversational cat. She loves to travel, camp at the lake, and spend time with friends.

Nancy Meyers Faltermeier writes non-fiction and Young Adult fantasy. In past years she worked full time with a ministry noted for the children's albums *Music Machine* and *Bullfrogs and Butterflies.* There she wrote skits, plays, and songs. Music she wrote, found publication in two songbooks and four recordings by different artists.

She has also taught Bible Studies on many different topics and levels. After homeschooling her children through high school, she is dedicating her time bringing hope to the hurting through the written word. Nancy resides at the base of the Rockies in beautiful Colorado with her husband, two adult children, two parakeets, and a backyard nursery of wild cottontail bunnies. In her spare time, she enjoys hiking, amateur photography, and scrapbooking.

Gone to unearth more truths for hurting hearts.